Art Nouveau
LAMPSHADES
& MIRRORS

Kim Fowler

Kangaroo Press

Thanks to the Lord Jesus for inspiring me.
You've been good to me. Thanks so much.

Acknowledgments

Many thanks to my parents, always a
source of encouragement. I love ya.

Lamp technique photography by
Bernard Terry of Nambour, Queensland.

First published in 1997 by Kangaroo Press Pty Ltd
An imprint of Simon & Schuster Australia
20 Barcoo Street (PO Box 507)
East Roseville NSW 2069 Australia
Printed in Hong Kong through Colorcraft Ltd

ISBN 0 86417 849 2

Contents

Introduction

In the 1890s an exotic new school of design known as Art Nouveau became popular in Europe, pushing away the past of the Victorian masters, the Renaissance, Baroque and Rococo styles of figurative realism which allowed no room for exploration.

Art Nouveau's beginnings can be traced back to the 1860s, to the influence of the artists of the Pre-Raphaelite Brotherhood—William Morris, Edward Burne-Jones, James McNeill, to name a few—who opened the way for acceptance of the sensuous, extravagant work of Aubrey Beardsley, Henri de Toulouse-Lautrec and Emile Gallé. Freed from realism, Art Nouveau's fresh romantic beauty was inspired by nature, by flora and fauna, the insect world, the female figure. The sinuous flowing lines of the designs were often linked by a graceful whiplash curve. Above all, Art Nouveau was easy on the eye.

The American designer Louis Comfort Tiffany added much to the applied art of the period with his work in stained glass. During his journeys to Europe he was inspired by the brilliance of the glass used in Mediaeval windows to set out on a quest to manufacture a glass that would not need to be painted and stained as heavily as the glass in use at the time. He created a beautiful opaque glass which needed very little surface treatment. Tiffany used his new glass in his famous lampshades and windows in designs typical of the Art Nouveau movement.

Art Nouveau's place in the sun was short-lived at the time, however. By the late 1920s the influences of industrialisation, the after-effects of World War I, and the Great Depression, combined to lead to functionalism in design replacing the extravagances of the style of the previous years. Despite this, Art Nouveau has had a far-reaching influence on design—its effects are seen to this day—maybe more than any other design movement in history. The style pervaded architecture, interiors, furniture, jewellery, glass; nearly everything you could imagine.

I find it interesting that stained glass was so readily accepted as art then—more so then than now. It would be lovely to see a greater use of leadlight in Australia; it can add a sparkle and an atmosphere to an interior that no other form of art can. Works in stained glass in restaurants and public buildings would bring art to people who would not think to visit a gallery; it would lift their senses and inspire them.

George Inness, an artist who greatly influenced Tiffany, taught from the belief that 'the true artistic impulse is divine'. If we could just harness that, we also could produce art that is fresh and ageless. Tiffany recognised what Inness was saying and the fruits of his realisation are obvious.

Kim Fowler

LAMPS

Tips and techniques for lampshades

Keeping these techniques and tips in mind will help you achieve a more professional finish to your work.

Use the variations and the colour in the glass to make your lampshade more interesting. Different textures of glass add another dimension. Choose the shape that you prefer, or that best suits your base; with that shape you can design your own lampshades to suit a particular room, the colours in the room, the period or any decor.

> **TIP:** When choosing glass, hold it in front of a normal household lightbulb, not a fluorescent light, to see its true colours.

1. CUTTING When cutting out the lamp, be as accurate as possible, making sure the outside edge of each panel is straight and just inside the edge line of each pattern piece. If you are not accurate, you will find when you place the pieces of glass in the jig that the sides are uneven, and the pieces will be either too small or too big. They will put the lampshade out of shape or leave you with large gaps between the seams. Accuracy always pays—your lamp will be symmetrical and well balanced.

> **TIP:** When breaking narrow pieces of glass, use two pairs of pliers—one to hold the narrow piece and the other to break. It works wonders.

2. GRINDING Grind and number each piece of glass corresponding to the numbered pattern, dry and wipe clean.

3. FOIL I like to use 5 mm (3/16") copperfoil (use black-backed for transparent glass). Use 6 mm (7/32") or 7 mm (1/4") foil for thicker glass.

Centre glass on foil, run foil around the edge, overlap and tear or cut off. Press sides over and burnish with a lathekin or pen. When the foil doesn't stick the most common causes are the glass not being clean or high atmospheric humidity.

4. Place the pattern on the bench and nail wooden bats just on the outside of the two vertical lines of the panel. Place your glass within the jig, adjusting if necessary.

5. SOLDERING TECHNIQUES Paint flux on all foil in sight except the two vertical outside edges. Then solder; don't play around in one area of your panel for too long or on pieces that are thin (tips of leaves, etc.) as the glass can become too hot and crack—disappointing when you're getting somewhere. Touch the glass to see if it is too hot. Move to the other end of the panel and go back when the glass has cooled a little.

Solder a raised bead (a smooth rounded seam) on the outside of the panel, raising it by adding more solder, then turn over and flat solder on the inside. As you get to know your soldering iron, your work will become neater. Don't despair at your work, because I guarantee as time goes by soldering will become second nature. DON'T drag the iron along the surface of your seam, that can make it look messy. Don't fear soldering but approach it with a sure hand.

To smooth out lumpy areas press iron down (to the glass) and up firmly. You can also run the soldering iron deftly along the seams, but make sure the tip of the iron is touching the glass and foil.

If the tip of the iron is pitted or damaged it will tear the foil. Always keep the tip filed smooth and tinned.

Have a container of water nearby to cool the iron by dipping the end of the tip into it.

If there is too much solder at one point, press

iron down firmly, take it up quickly and flick it so the excess drops off. Soldering will never be perfect, so if you are getting frustrated, go for a walk or have a cup of tea or both!

Solder all panels, wash with whiting or dish-washing liquid, rub numbers off with towelling, and dry. If you don't finish soldering all the panels by the end of the day, wash the ones that you have finished. Never leave flux on glass overnight as it will leave stains—always wash it off.

Soldering a lamp together, cleaning and applying patina should be done over one or two days at the most, as the patina will take more evenly.

> **TIP:** I use Baker's or Radiant solder fluid for all soldering (copper and lead) except around mirror joints, where tallow candle is used. This is a personal choice; there are many other fluxes on the market. I use 60–40 solder for all soldering.

6. FORMING A CONE Place panels side by side leaving 1 mm between panels. (When working with lampshades with only 4 to 6 panels, leave 1–2 mm space so the panels won't be too tight when pulled up to the cone position.) Apply heaps of masking tape or sticky tape. Overlap the tape with a ring of tape going around the top, bottom and middle if necessary. Don't scrimp on the tape—better to overdo it than underdo it, as the lamp could collapse and you would find yourself starting again. So rule 1: make sure glass is very clean and don't scrimp on tape. In humid climates foil and cone indoors or near a fan.

Pulling lamp towards your body and letting the edge of it lean against you, pull the lamp up (Figure 1, page 17) so that edges meet, and secure with tape. Check to see that panels are meeting correctly at top and bottom of all seams and that the edges are sitting flat on the table. Flux all top and bottom joins and tack-solder.

7. VASE CAP Flux and solder lightly around edge of cap, sit the vase cap on top of the lamp, check to see that it is sitting straight and centred, and tack-solder to the seams. This gives the lamp a lot of strength. Try different caps to see which suits best. If there are big gaps between the rim and the lamp just solder the cap at the top of the seams to start with. Later on, when you turn the lamp over to do the inside seams, apply masking tape over the gaps between the cap and glass panels, so when you finish soldering the cap on the outside the solder will not drip through. Usually with 6- or 8-sided lamps I only solder the cap at the top of the seam anyway. When the wire is soldered around at the bottom the lampshade will be strong enough—use your judgement.

> **TIP:** Some caps will take patina straight away and go black; if not, another technique you can try is adding salt to your patina (not in your bottle!). Apply with a cotton ball soaked with the solution; if this fails you need to apply clean flux, rubbing in well. Take a little solder and start spreading it around, working it in a circular motion. If it's streaky or lumpy, too much solder has been applied (see 5, Soldering techniques). And the other alternative is to leave the cap brass and polish with Brasso.

8. SOLDERING SEAMS Solder blobs of solder all the way down each seam (Figure 2, page 17). If the solder begins to run, move further down the seam and come back later. Keep on applying solder until you can't see any daylight between seams. This means that when you smooth the solder out, you won't have to apply much more to achieve a nicely rounded seam.

Turn the lamp over and lay it on the bench, then solder the seam that is closest to the bench. Solder all seams, rotating the lamp as you go. When they are done, turn lamp over.

Hold the lamp so that the seam you are working on is horizontal to the bench (see Figure 3, page 17). Hold the lamp very still and finish off the seam by making a nice rounded bead (see 5, Soldering techniques). When all seams are beaded, place the lamp on a folded towel or some thick sponge and run copper wire around the bottom (see Figure 4, page 17). Stretch the wire over your flux brush to remove any kinks, tack-solder and continue to press the wire against the rim of the lamp, tacking as you go, and overlapping at the end. Cut with leadcutters then go back around and bead-solder.

9. CLEANING AND POLISHING Clean the lamp, with whiting, water and a piece of towelling. Rinse. Patina with a fine paintbrush or cottonbud, trying not to let any patina touch the glass (it is inevitable but beware) as patina can leave faint marks on the glass that are permanent. Continue to run water over the lamp as you go. Patina inside as well. Clean patina off with whiting and water, then towel dry. Apply stove-black polish with a toothbrush, paying attention to all soldered areas, and polish with a soft brush. Sometimes there will be excess polish smeared on the glass—

if you need to, dampen a cloth and wipe the glass only—then finito, finished!

10. REPAIRING If you break a piece of glass during construction of your lampshade it's easier to repair it once the lamp is completed. These instructions apply to any broken glass in a foiled project. Score the surface of the broken piece, criss-crossing it in all directions, then with safety glasses on, tap the underside of the glass with the end of your glass-cutter. The glass will crack and fly about (hence the safety glasses). Remove as much broken glass as you can with pliers or tweezers. Heat up the soldering iron, apply flux to the solder which was around the broken piece, and melt it out. Find the end of the piece of foil which was around the broken glass and pull the foil away from the lamp at the same time, smooth, cut a new piece of glass and replace.

TIP: Because of the distortions which can occur during photocopying, always check your patterns before cutting. The outside lines of an individual panel are the most important—they must be symmetrical.

SAFETY

1. Always solder in a well-ventilated area, preferably in front of an extraction fan. If this is not possible, place a fan near you, side-on to the bench, to create a stream of air between you and the lampshade to blow the fumes away before you breathe them in. Remember, solder fumes are toxic and can lodge in your body, so be wise.

2. Always wear gloves while soldering, cleaning and working with patina. I use the very thin disposable gloves available in supermarkets.

Waratahs

Illustrated on inside front cover

12 panels
115 mm (4½") vented lace heat vase cap
Lady Diana base 324 mm (12¾") high

I used apricot wispy Iridized glass for the main body, cherry red Corella Cathedral for the flower petals and red amber Streaky Granite for the tops of the flowers, which was just the right combination of glass to achieve the effect I wanted.

Three hot colours were used around the bottom edge: pink and red Muffle and mauve Wavolite (or Artico).

join

ENLARGE AT 200%
(2 cm = 4 cm; 1″ = 2″)

join

Study in pale pink

Illustrated on inside front cover

7 panels
65 mm (2½") vase cap
230 mm (9") high; 260 mm (10¼") wide
Lady Diana lamp base 324 mm (12¾") high
7 ice-drop crystals 20 mm (¾")
14 teardrop crystals 15 mm (½")

My client wanted something feminine and different, and I think we achieved that. This is an eye-catching lamp, with the crystals shimmering along the bottom making it really special. Solder U-shaped copper hooks around the bottom of the lamp in the places marked X. I used the larger crystal in the middle and two smaller ones either side.

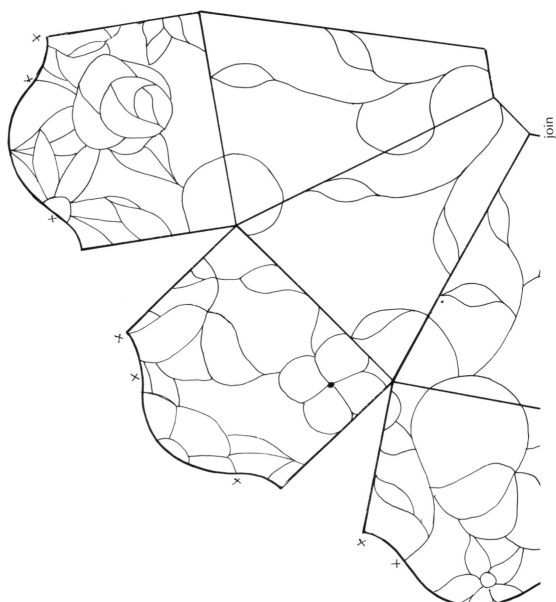

join

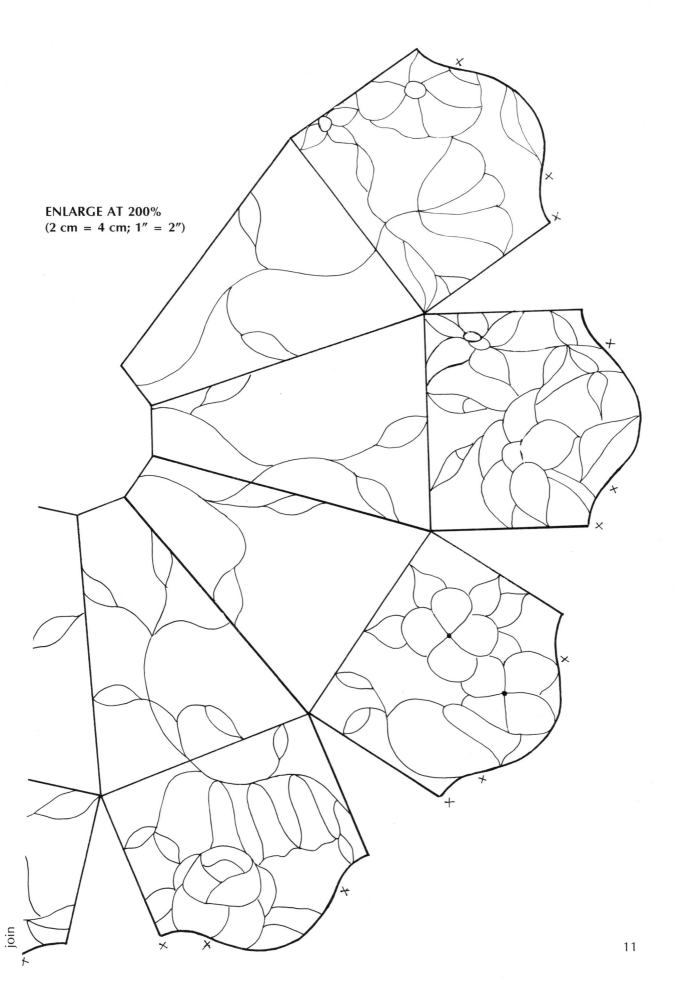

ENLARGE AT 200%
(2 cm = 4 cm; 1″ = 2″)

join

Classic Australian pendant lamp

Illustrated on page 18

10 panels
75 mm (3") split vented vase cap
210 mm (8¼") high; 450 mm (17¾") wide

Cut 5 panels from the pattern, and repeat. Note: The curved shape at the top of the panels must be reversed to match the shapes on the repeat.

This is a fabulous lamp which will never date.

ENLARGE AT 125%
(4 cm = 5 cm; 2" = 2½")

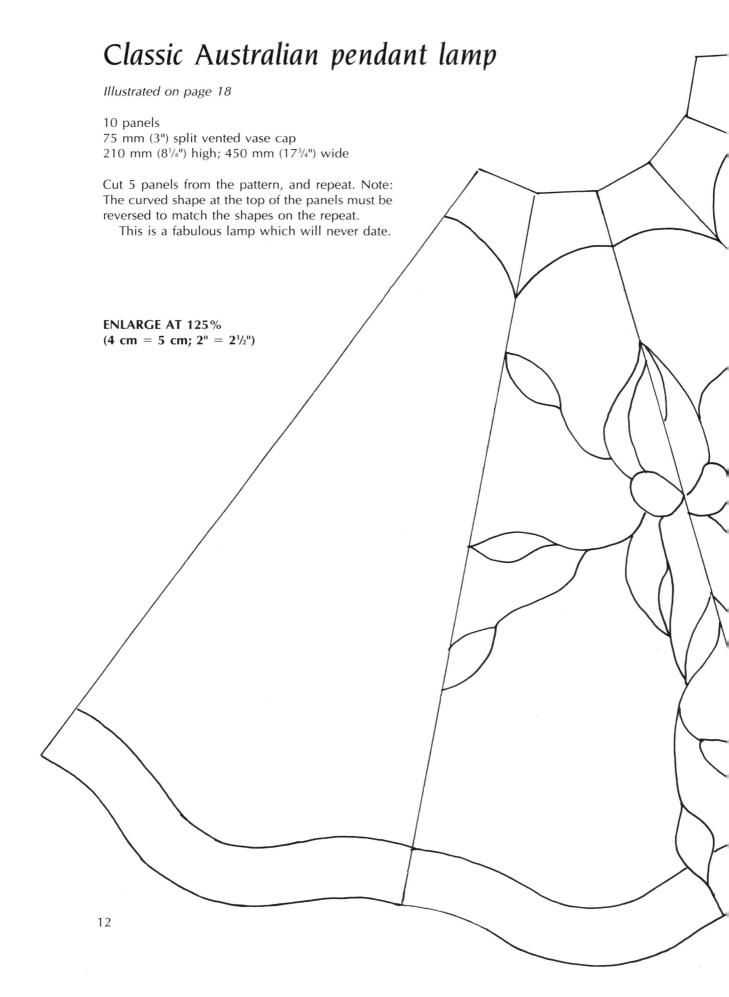

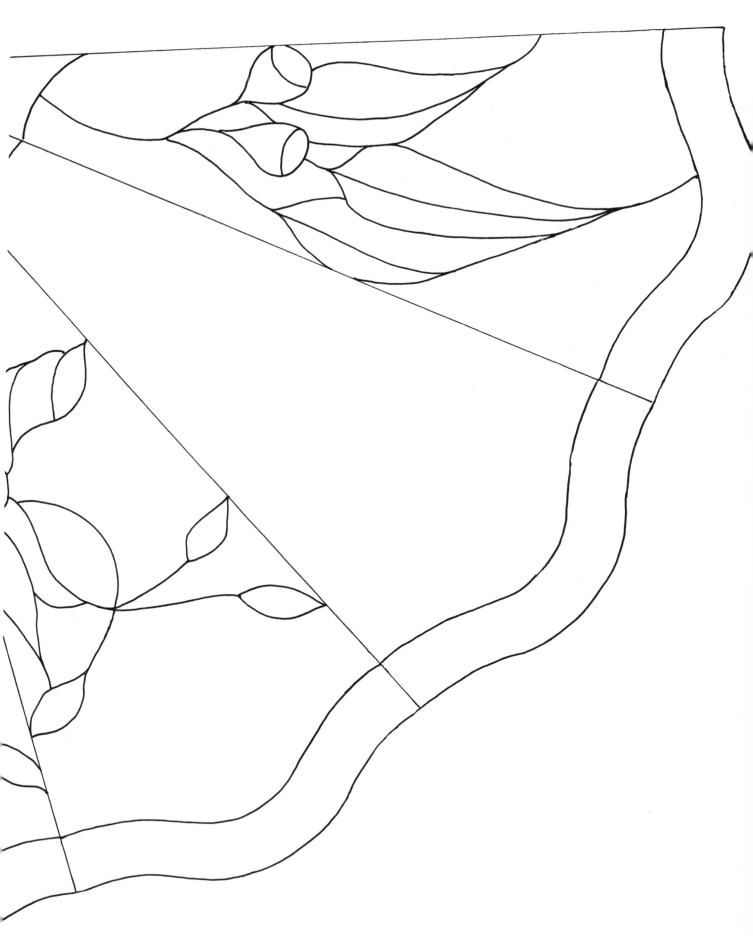

Petite lady's lamp

Illustrated on page 18

6 panels
50 mm (2") vase cap
135 mm (5¼") high
Bowery lamp base 150 mm (5½") high

Cut the glass larger than actual pattern size to allow for shrinkage in kiln. Paint a sinuous vine along bottom of panels with gold paint suitable for firing (up to 840°C/1544°F), place tiny leaves onto the vine and when gold paint is dry place on prepared kiln shelf. It is a good idea to make up an extra panel in case of any breakages. Don't take leaves right to bottom edge of panel, but leave enough room to adhere the foil.

ACTUAL SIZE

Fleur-de-lis

Illustrated on page 18

6 panels
Bowery lamp base 140 mm (5½") high

Use two pairs of pliers to break those small side
pieces.

ACTUAL SIZE

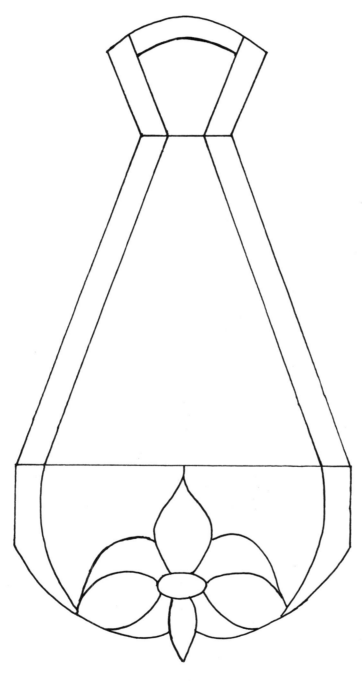

Nouveau roses

Illustrated on inside front cover

12 panels
130 mm (5") vase cap
230 mm (9") high; 460 mm (18") wide
Fluted lamp base 334 mm (13") high

This is definitely my favourite.

I was tempted to design the roses more simply but detail makes the design. Iridized pink spectrum for the main body and apricot white wispy iridized, red muffle and violet Wavolite (or Artico) were perfect for the roses. The lamp was finished off with U-shaped brass filigree banding around the bottom soldered in place.

This pattern appears full-size on the fold-out pattern sheet.

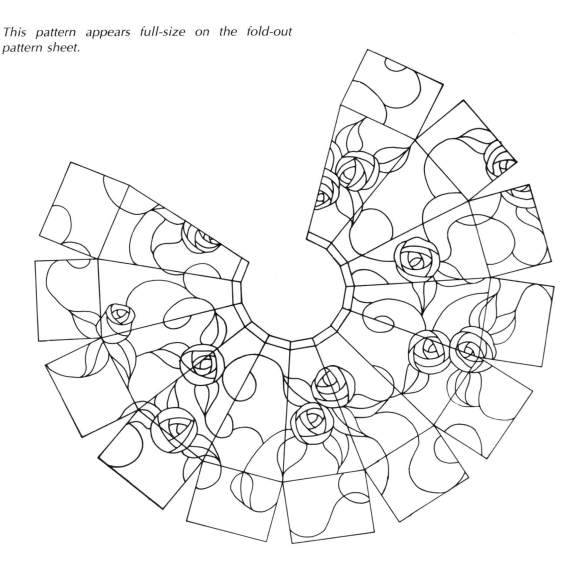

FORMING A CONE (page 10)

Figure 1   *Use plenty of tape to hold the lamp together*

SOLDERING SEAMS (page 10)

Figure 2   *Solder blobs of solder all the way down each seam*

Figure 3   *With the seam you are working on horizontal to the bench, finish off the seam with a nice rounded bead*

Note: *The seams are not bead-soldered as they should be, as I skipped a couple of steps for the purpose of photographing this stage of the lamp's construction*

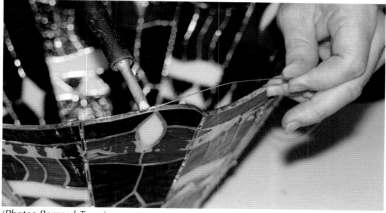

(Photos Bernard Terry)

Figure 4   *When all the seams are beaded, run copper wire around the bottom of the lampshade*

RIGHT: *Petite lady's lamp (page 14)*

BELOW: *Classic Australian pendant lamp (page 12)*

ABOVE: *Fan lamp in pale pink (page 19)*

LEFT: *Fleur-de-lis lamp (page 15)*

18

Fan lamp in pale pink

Illustrated on page 18

This lamp matches Study in Pale Pink, illustrated on the inside front cover.

Flemish fan base

You might have to solder small blobs to the back of the fan to ensure that it sits straight.

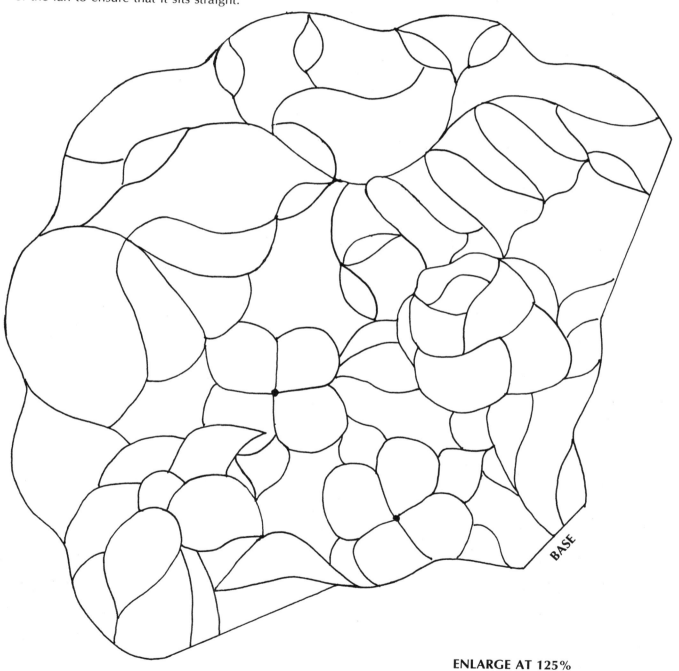

BASE

ENLARGE AT 125%
(4 cm = 5 cm; 2" = 2½")

Little jewel

Illustrated on page 35

6 panels
Bowery lamp base 140 mm (5½") high

I chose pink clear Uroborous glass for this little
lamp, with red Flemish trim. The photo doesn't do
this one justice—it was good enough to eat!

ACTUAL SIZE

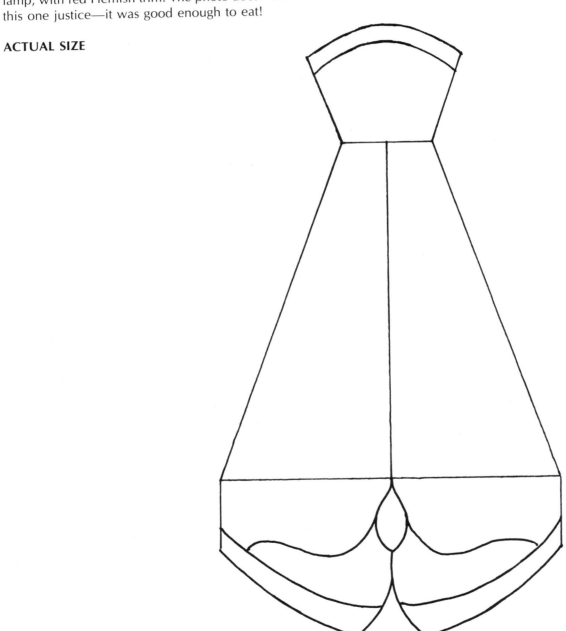

Daffodil

Illustrated on page 35

12 panels
Small lily lamp base 191 mm (7½") high

I could not purchase a vase cap to fit the proportions of this lamp so I cut a cap to size with tin snips. I like the design. This would be a stylish pendant lamp in the right setting.

ENLARGE TO SIZE REQUIRED

Seashells

Illustrated on page 35

9 panels
76 mm (3") cast brass vented cap
190 mm (7½") high; 390 mm (15½") wide
L313 lamp base

ACTUAL SIZE

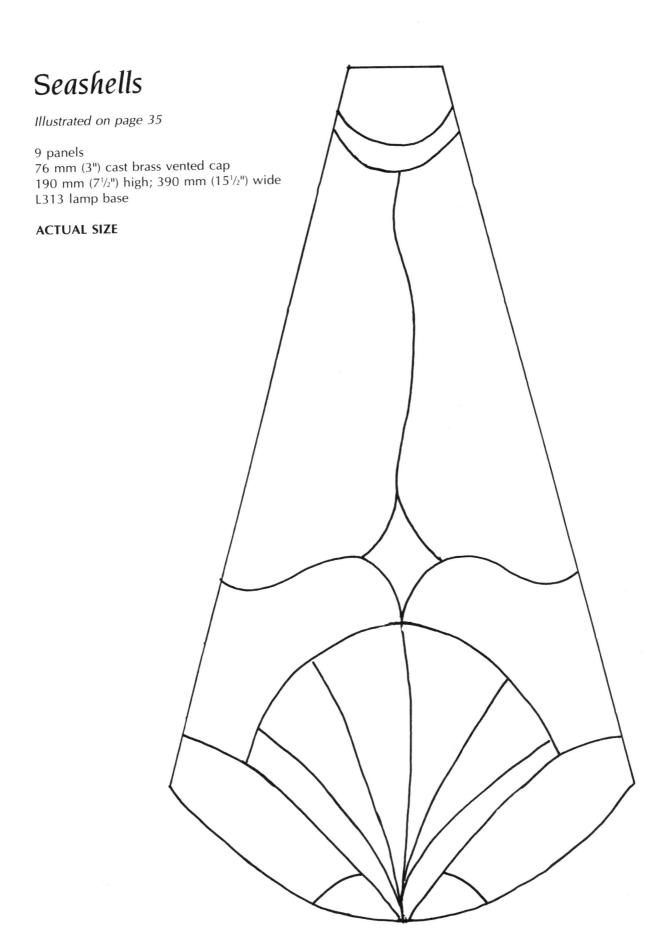

Floral belle

Illustrated on page 35

9 panels
190 mm (7½") high; 280 mm (11") wide
Brass clover lamp base 229 mm (11¾") high

I could not purchase a cap to fit, so I had to cut a cap to fit with tin snips. After completely assembling lamp, cut centre of flower to fit, foil and solder in place.

ACTUAL SIZE

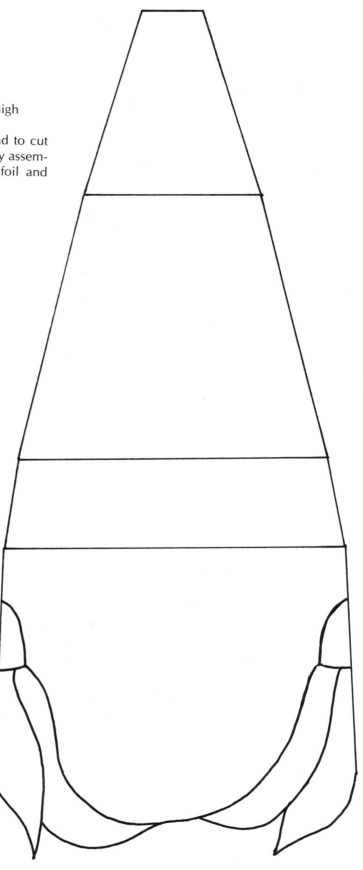

Simple bejewelled bedside lamp

Illustrated on page 36

4 panels
L313 lamp base

I made a pair in this design, in white as my client
wanted to be able to read by them. I also added
some pieces of glass plate to the centre jewelled
area to achieve the right effect. Bullseye is also a
great glass for the main body in this lamp.

ENLARGE AT 125%
(4 cm = 5 cm; 2" = 2½")

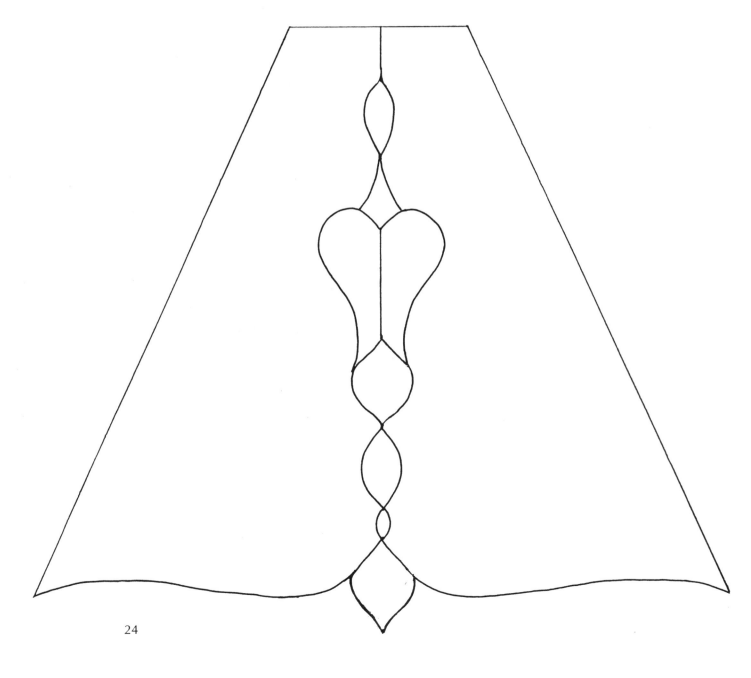

Kaleidoscope

Illustrated on page 36

14 panels
114 mm (4½") vented lace heat cap
210 mm (8¼") high; 350 mm (13¾") wide
Nouveau lamp base 273 mm (10¾") high

Another favourite!
    I chose blue-green clear Wavolite for the main body of this lamp, which is unsurpassed. This lamp really glows.
    Cut 7 each panels of A and B.

ACTUAL SIZE

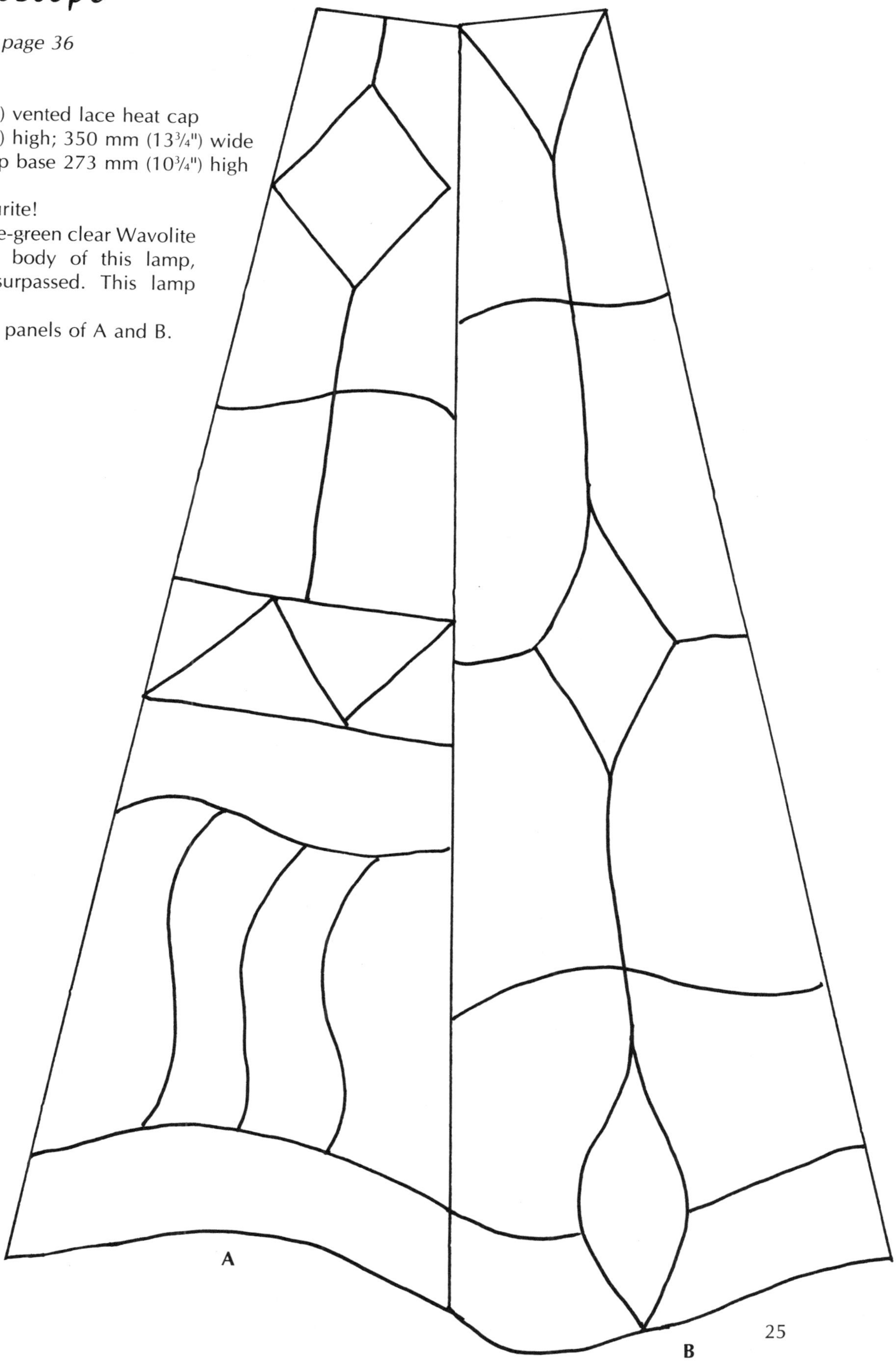

A

B

25

Patricia's standard

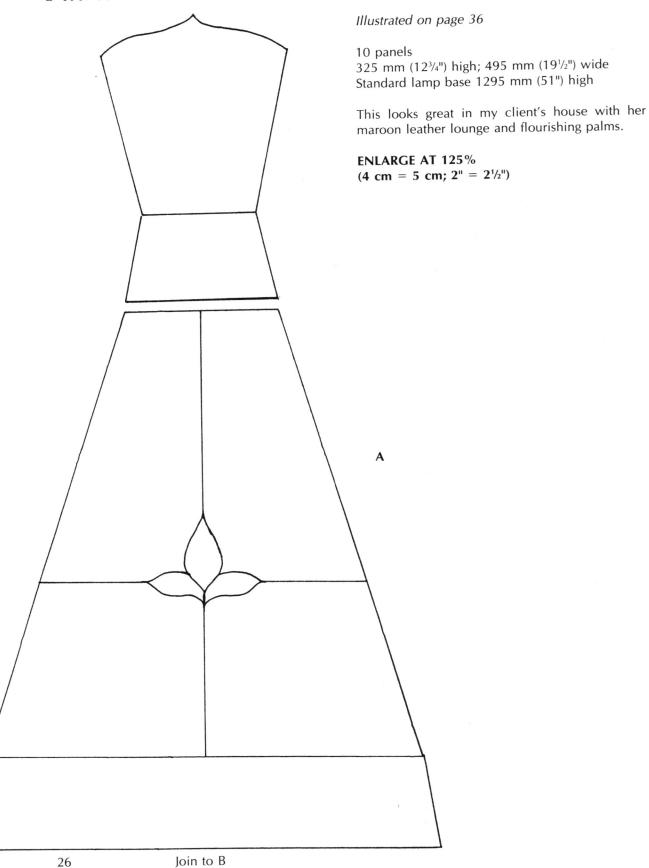

Illustrated on page 36

10 panels
325 mm (12¾") high; 495 mm (19½") wide
Standard lamp base 1295 mm (51") high

This looks great in my client's house with her maroon leather lounge and flourishing palms.

ENLARGE AT 125%
(4 cm = 5 cm; 2" = 2½")

A

Join to B

Join to A

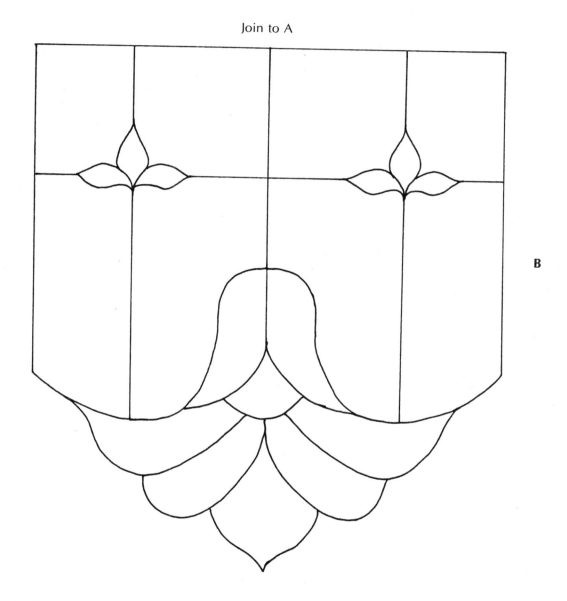

B

ENLARGE AT 125%
(4 cm = 5 cm; 2" = 2½")

Poppy buds

Illustrated on page 36

12 panels
76 mm (3") vase cap
190 mm (7½") high; 360 mm (14") wide
L303 lamp base, 206 mm (8") high

A medium size lamp, specially designed to match the owner's Sheridan quilt and curtains. Cut 2 sets of the 6 panels. Solder the main body in jig, then the skirt in the jig also.

I like the way the leaves flow around the bottom.

ENLARGE AT 125%
(4 cm = 5 cm; 2" = 2½")

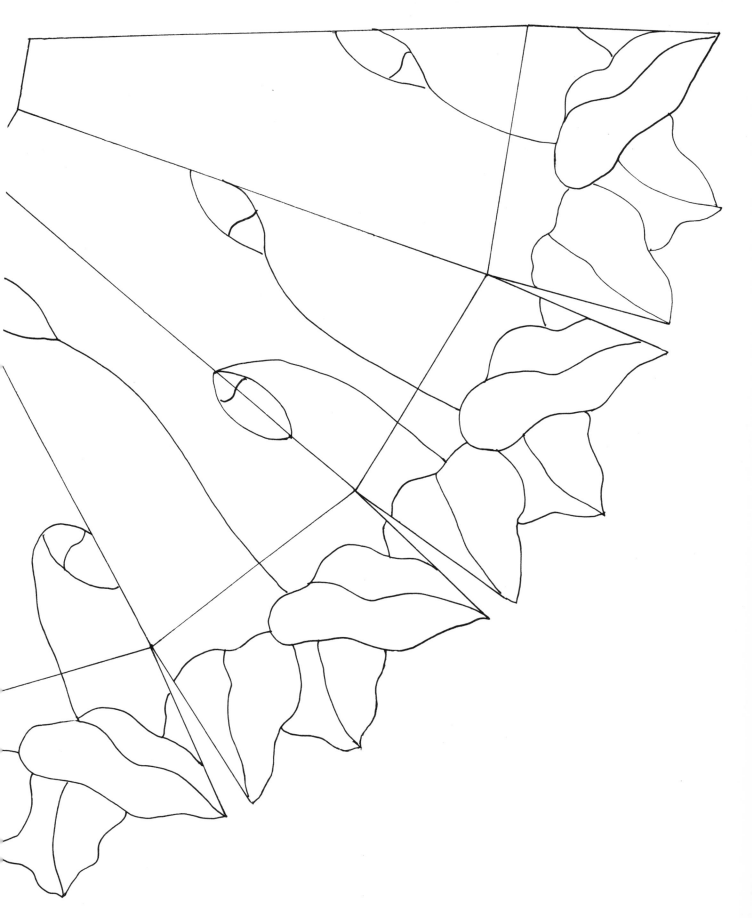

Japanese lanterns

Illustrated on page 37

10 panels
210 mm (8¼") wide; 310 mm (12") high
100 mm (4") black beaded fringing
U-shaped filigree brass banding
thin galvanised iron

My absolute favourite (I think!) An absolutely exotic lamp (a bit like the owners, my favourite picture framers, Edwin and Birgette Salzmann of Nhulunbuy in the Northern Territory). 'Japanese lanterns' refers to the flower of that name.

Place panels side by side and tape well. Cone and place on bench with the top of lamp on the bench (upside down). Check to see that all angles at seams are similar (check top and bottom of lamp), tack solder, and place as much solder in seams as possible to make the lamp as stable as possible. Place the lamp upright on the sheet of thin galvanised iron, mark the outline and cut with tin snips or an angle grinder. Smooth edges and tin, following the instructions for coach-lamps on the next page. Turn lamp right way up and solder to lid. Clean, patina, etc. Now you are ready to add the fringe. Check out bead or haberdashery shops for suitable beaded fringing.

Take band and fold into thirds along dotted lines shown in Figure 1 into the shape shown in Figure 2, iron and stitch to secure, then place band inside U-shaped brass banding cut to exact circumference of the bottom of lamp. Make sure the band of beading is straight, then clamp the brass banding down with pliers, tack onto a few places around bottom of lamp and solder, joining ends together neatly. Wipe off flux (by the way, use flux sparingly here) and paint brass band carefully with flat black Rustguard paint. Paint the top of the lamp too. Polish.

ENLARGE AT 125%
(4 cm = 5 cm; 2" = 2½")

Figure 1   Figure 2

COACHLAMPS

Tips for coachlamps

1. Foil and solder each of the four panels in a jig. Position and solder square U lead around each panel. Patina and clean.

2. Tin outside edge on both sides of 165 mm (6½") square galvanised iron lid. Persevere with this. Sand well before tinning and smooth off.

3. Tack-solder four panels into a square as shown in the bird's-eye view of the corners. Check with L-square. Solder top, middle and bottom. Then solder lid to panels, solder around edges and smooth off.

4. Paint lid with flat black Rust-guard, clean and polish all over.

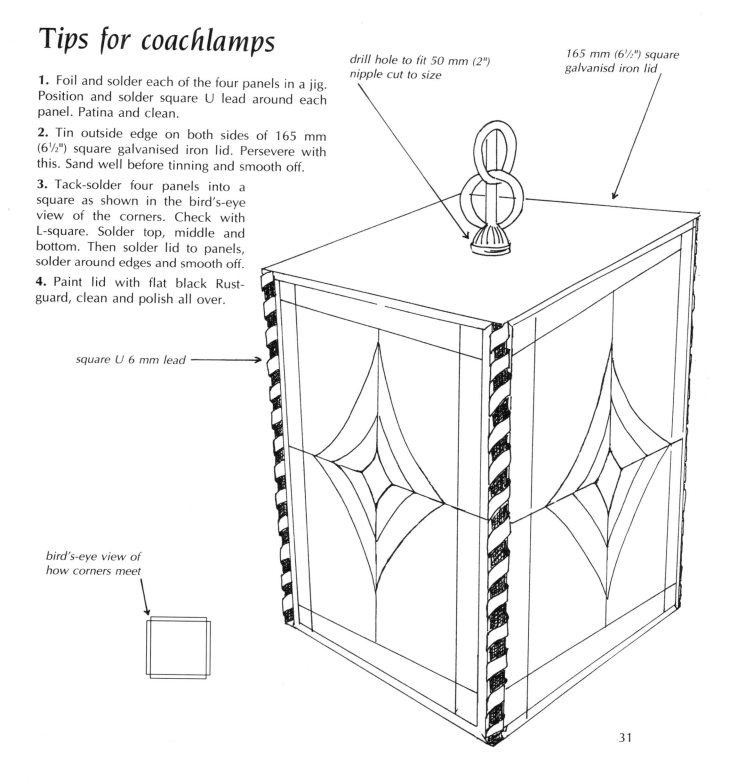

drill hole to fit 50 mm (2") nipple cut to size

165 mm (6½") square galvanisd iron lid

square U 6 mm lead

bird's-eye view of how corners meet

Istanbul

Illustrated on page 37

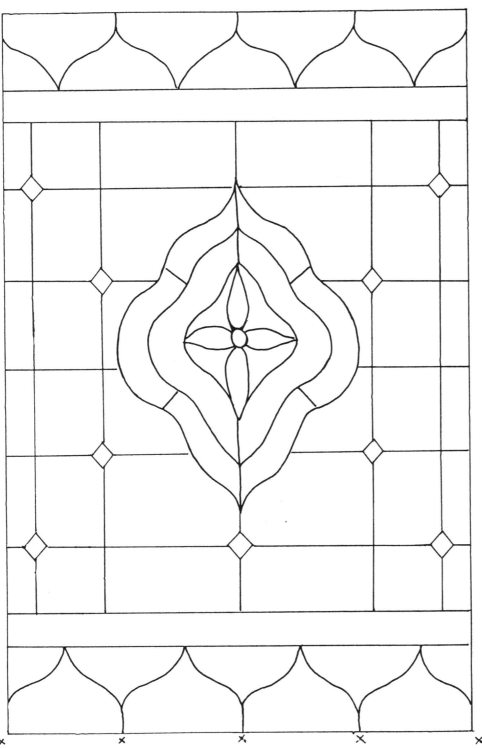

My favourite (really)!

This one is a lot of work but worth it. If you can't get crystals with holes at the top and bottom (I added a dark blue glass bead to the bottom of each crystal), it doesn't matter—just hang a normal crystal which will look fantastic. Solder U-shaped copper wire hooks from the points marked X.

ENLARGE AT 125%
(4 cm = 5 cm; 2" = 2½")

Flower lamp

Illustrated on page 37

I used dark green uroborous glass at top and bottom; the combination of this with grape waterglass, red and amber in the circles and bottom band pattern, plus the multi-coloured flower petal, gave this lamp a rich, opulent feel. The crystals are 20 mm (³⁄₈") ice-drops. Solder U-shaped hooks at the points marked X.

ENLARGE AT 125%
(4 cm = 5 cm; 2" = 2½")

Palace courtyard

Illustrated on page 37

A quite simple but effective lamp using different textured clear glass. I really liked the outside edge glass that has a large round hammered pattern on it. It is an old glass and quite common—check out demolition yards for this one.

I bent flat brass 20 mm gallery edging to shape, placed it right on the bottom edge of the lead and soldered it into place. These brass edgings are great and easy to work with, and add interest. Patina the brass with salt and patina.

ENLARGE AT 125%
(4 cm = 5 cm; 2" = 2½")

ABOVE: *Little jewel lamp (page 20)*

ABOVE RIGHT: *Daffodil lamp (page 21)*

BELOW RIGHT: *Floral belle lamp (page 23)*

Seashells lamp (page 22)

Pair of simple bejewelled bedside lamps (page 24)

RIGHT: *Kaleidoscope lamp (page 25)*

Patricia's standard lamp (page 26)

Poppy buds lamp (page 28)

ABOVE: *Japanese lanterns lamp (page 30)*
ABOVE RIGHT: *Istanbul coachlamp (page 32)*

BELOW: *Flower coachlamp (page 33)*
BELOW RIGHT: *Palace courtyard coachlamp (page 34)*

Nautical coachlamp (page 40)
Turkish delight coachlamp (page 43)

Hearts and leaves coachlamp (page 39)
Oriental rose coachlamp (page 42)

Hearts and leaves

Illustrated opposite

Rose red ripple, amber ripple, iridized olive green Corella Cathedral, red Flemish hearts, a touch of floral clear at the top and some moulded leaves found years ago and treasured (which could be replaced effectively by lime green white translucent).

Solder hooks to points marked X. I foiled red nuggets, then soldered copper wire around them and hung them on the four corners with beads added threaded on eye-pins (bought at bead shops). I placed beads on eye-pins at the other points marked X. Then I took a long string of maroon and amber glass beads and draped them around the lamp, hooking it evenly into the tops of the eye-pins. The curly bits in the hearts (which didn't come out in the photograph) are copper wire bent and soldered into place.

ENLARGE AT 125%
(4 cm = 5 cm; 2" = 2½")

Nautical coachlamp

Illustrated on page 38

Sides 1 and 3 show the sailing ship
Side 2 shows flag 'Zulu/Shore station'
Side 4 shows flag 'Charlie/Yes/Affirmative'

Replace the centre panel of the sailing ship with the flag panels for the second and fourth sides.

ENLARGE AT 125%
(4 cm = 5 cm; 2" = 2½")

Sides 1 and 3

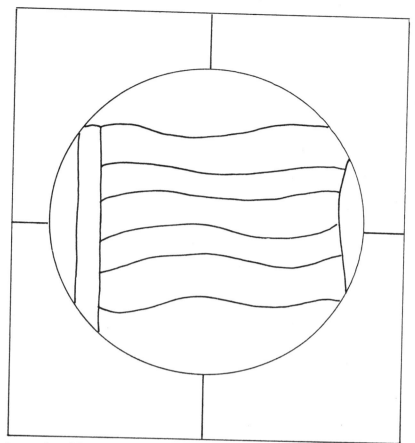

ENLARGE AT 125%
(4 cm = 5 cm; 2" = 2½")

Insert for side 2

ENLARGE AT 125%
(4 cm = 5 cm; 2" = 2½")

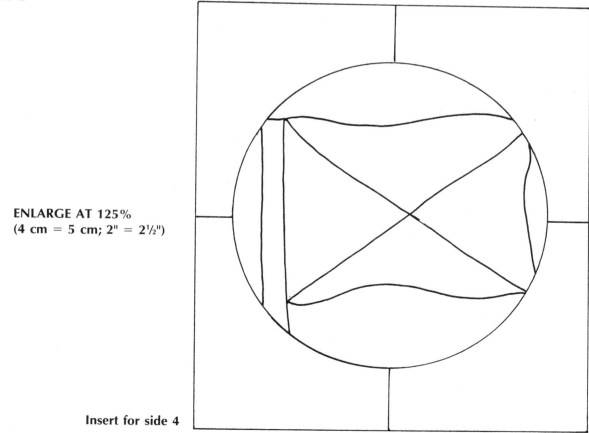

Insert for side 4

Oriental rose

Illustrated on page 38

I love this one. The friend who bought it hung it over her bed which has a beautiful hand-made red and blue Chinese silk patchwork bedspread.

This lamp is a lot of work but it truly is worth it. I love the combination of the iridized amber ripple and the red Flemish glass with the delicacy of the background flowers, set in light pink glue chip. I'd love to enlarge this for a large port-hole window.

ENLARGE AT 125%
(4 cm = 5 cm; 2" = 2½")

Turkish delight

Illustrated on page 38

18 panels top
18 panels bottom
165 mm (6½") wide; 300 mm (12") high
2 x 100 mm (4") fluted brass caps
2 brass hinges 30 mm x 20 mm (1¼" x ¾"); you don't need the bottom pieces
35 mm (1½") pendant brass finial, screwed onto threaded nipple and cut to size; place in opening of fluted brass cap and secure with a brass locknut on inside of cap—this is for bottom section of lamp
38 mm (1½") cast brass loop (for hanging top section)

I used gold-pink ripple, red Flemish, tight orange ripple, medium purple waterglass, cherry-red Corella Cathedral, and tight orange ripple placed in that order. I cut 6 of each colour, making 36 pieces, enough for both top and bottom sections.

Foil, lay out, tape and cone both sections. Use the 152 mm (6") circle as your guide to achieving an even circle. Solder vase caps. Join the two sections at the middle and check to ensure they are meeting evenly—fiddly, but necessary—before soldering seams in position. Clean, patina, polish. Slightly bend brass hinges to take in the curve of the lamp, flux and solder to bottom rim of top section of lamp (Figure 1). Solder as securely as possible.

ACTUAL SIZE

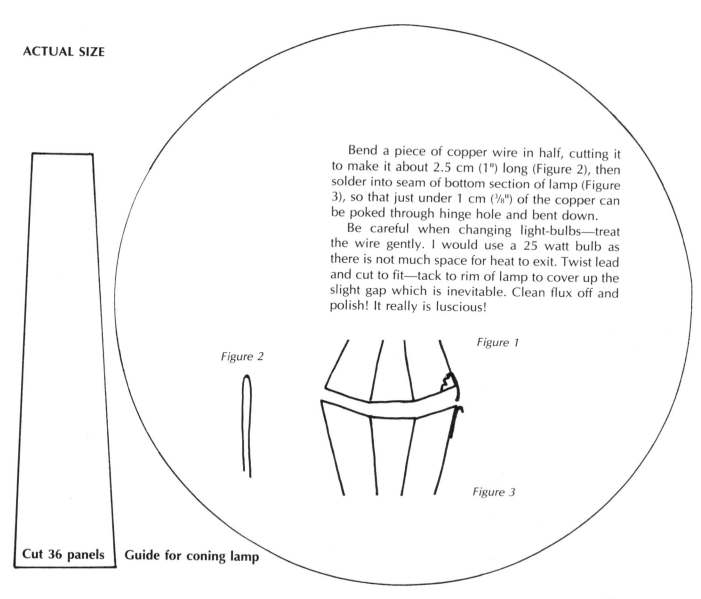

Bend a piece of copper wire in half, cutting it to make it about 2.5 cm (1") long (Figure 2), then solder into seam of bottom section of lamp (Figure 3), so that just under 1 cm (³/₈") of the copper can be poked through hinge hole and bent down.

Be careful when changing light-bulbs—treat the wire gently. I would use a 25 watt bulb as there is not much space for heat to exit. Twist lead and cut to fit—tack to rim of lamp to cover up the slight gap which is inevitable. Clean flux off and polish! It really is luscious!

Figure 2

Figure 1

Figure 3

Cut 36 panels | Guide for coning lamp

MIRRORS

Tips for leadlight mirrors

I will be brief here as there are many books fully describing leading techniques.

Leadlight mirrors really catch the eye, especially if you have chosen strong colours—although plain mirror and lead look great if you have the right design. Opaque and iridized glass work well. If you have chosen transparent glass for parts of your mirror, place white paper behind those parts before adding backing. And just the right frame will really set your mirror off.

1. Treat mirrored glass with respect, being very careful that you don't scratch the silver off the back of it. Score on the front mirror surface, cut on a towel and shake off any slivers of glass.

2. I prefer to surround mirror glass only with lead as, due to the acid in flux, black spotting can sometimes appear on the edge of the mirror. If you do want to use foil around the edge there are many different fluxes on the market that you could try. Apply nail varnish or a recommended paint from a glass supplier around the edges of the mirror and use non-toxic flux, tallow candle or whatever your leadlight supplier advises you to use. Make a sample and let it sit for a week or two, then check for black spots. Use tallow candle on any lead joints adjacent to your mirror, giving them a good scrub first with a metal brush. You can use your normal flux for the rest of your mirror.

3. Black solder joints: To make black solder joints, putty, trim, then give your mirror a good scrub (paying attention to the joints) with a bristle brush and a small amount of whiting. Apply stove-black polish sparingly with toothbrush and buff lightly. If joints become silver again, scrub again with hard brush. Do this as soon as you have finished soldering your mirror.

Fusing

Fusing, which I have used on the Geckos mirror and the Mexico mirror, is another aspect of glasswork that can be quite addictive! I will be brief as there are books specifically published on this subject.

It is amazing how shiny and fluid-looking glass becomes after it has been fused; take a red Spectrum, for instance—you would think that it is shiny already but after it is fused and you've added some gold paint—*voila*! you really have something good enough to eat.

I found I had to be persistent with fusing. Glass cracking in the kiln, or after cooling, is inevitable, so you have to keep on—don't give up! That is the only way you can learn to know your kiln (where the hotter spots are, etc.) and your glass; which glass can be fused with which other (technical term, 'compatible').

So far I have only made earrings, necklaces, mirror surrounds, glass tiles and wonderful little bowls with fluid uneven sides the size of a saucer that can be used for sambals, jams or jewellery. I paint quirky sayings on these little bowls such as 'Let's have a jam' (on jam bowls) or 'On her Majesty's Service' (for jewellery). An arty, different cake plate is hard to find; personalise them for your customers or friends. Once you start the ideas keep coming; fused glass can be incorporated in leaded or foiled panels, fused glass pieces can be made to hang from suncatchers or lampshades.

Your glass supplier can give you an idea of which glass is compatible with which, such as Uroborous and Bullseye. There is a good numbering system, but making test samples first helps you to become familiar with the glass and will build up your knowledge of fusing. Place 25 mm x 200 mm (1" x 8") strips of glass in the kiln in colours you like, placing 12 mm (½") squares at intervals on top. Use Spectrum with Spectrum, etc. unless your supplier can advise you otherwise. After you have fused these samples you will see which will not adhere properly, which need to be sprayed with devitrifying spray (for glass that has a crystallized or dull surface after firing). Take notes.

BASIC PROCESS

1. With sandpaper rub off old kiln wash from your kiln shelves and paint the shelves with fresh kiln wash with a large soft brush four times in opposite directions (letting it dry between each coat). Make sure it is completely dry before smoothing with very find sandpaper or your hand. The same treatment is used on moulds for slumping.

2. Place clean glass on mould or kiln shelf (spray glass with devitrifying spray before you place it in the kiln if you already know that it needs it), care-fully close up kiln, checking to see that you haven't knocked any of your design out of place.

3. Switch kiln on to Low then slowly building up the temperature every half hour, take 2 hours to reach 520–540°C (968–1004°F) *Note:* Between 200–400°C (392–752°F) open kiln quickly (for 5 seconds) to let our moisture (i.e. flash vent). After reaching 540°C (1004°F) turn kiln up to High until you reach about 820–840°C (1508–1544°F). Now here you really have to keep an eye on it: glass has to soak at this temperature. Don't let the temperature rise higher; if you do, glass that is in a mould will start to melt and drip to the shelf or recede into the mould. Check continually through your spy-hole. When you see edges begin to become shiny and rounded, open or vent the kiln and let the temperature drop to 540°C (1004°F), then close kiln up and switch off. When it is cool check it out (if you can wait that long!). You can take your work out safely around 100°C (212°F).

These directions are for simple designs, with little pieces to be fused on top of your base glass piece, or pieces which can be slumped in a mould in one sitting. If you have a fair amount of glass that you want to fuse on top, the best idea would be to fuse this on the kiln shelf first, then the next day placing it on the mould and slumping.

Kimono mirror

Illustrated on inside back cover

This mirror really has a rich feel to it, and has been very popular. The flowers have been made with amber iridized ripple glass (again!—I love this glass) and when the light catches them they sparkle. Foil all flowers and the edges of the glass pieces immediately next to them and solder; patina, clean and then lead up.

This pattern appears full-size on the fold-out pattern sheet.

Navajo blanket mirror

Illustrated on page 55

I drew the lines for this mirror freehand to give it a rustic rather than a precise feeling, and I'm very happy with the effect. Hung above an antique sideboard this mirror would be eyecatching, to say the least.

ENLARGE BY 200-220%
(2 cm = 4-4.4 cm; 1" = 2-2¼" approx.)

join

**Blue and white
Indian mirror**

Illustrated on page 55

Securely solder hooks on the back of mirror.
Cover back of mirror with felt Contact cut to fit to
protect mirror backing from scratches.

ACTUAL SIZE

Whispering geckos

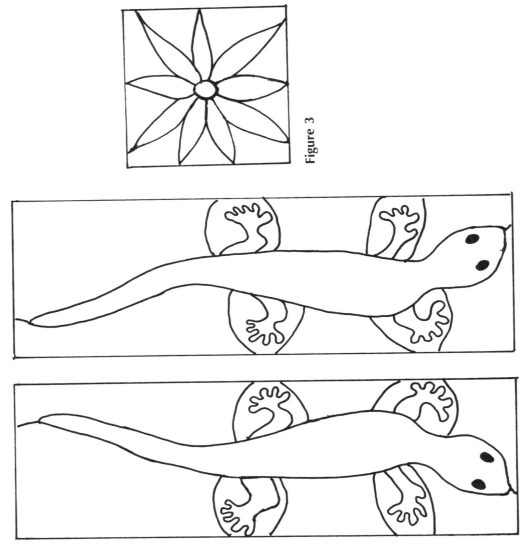

Figure 3

Figure 2

Figure 1

Illustrated on page 55

I haven't given you an actual mirror pattern here—it's up to you to choose the size you want, to choose the border width and enlarge the geckos to suit, if necessary. I wouldn't advise making them any smaller. My mirror is square, so the instructions are for a square mirror.

Draw up your pattern (you must do this, even though the border looks so simple, as you will have problems when leading if you don't). Make the border the width of the geckos and as long as 4 geckos and 2 flowers (with space in between every piece for the heart of your lead.)

Cut 8 geckos from Figure 1, 8 from Figure 2, and 4 flowers from Figure 3.

Because the leaf-shaped areas around the geckos' feet were stained with tracing black, like the eyes, I chose black waterglass for the main background colour.

Paint geckos' feet and eyes with tracing black mixed with gum arabic, vinegar and water. Mix well, grinding the lumps, paint onto very clean surface; when dry place geckos on prepared kiln shelf. You can fire quickly up to 600°C (1112°F), watching when the kiln gets near the desired temperature. When the paint looks shiny, turn kiln off.

Mexico

Illustrated on page 55

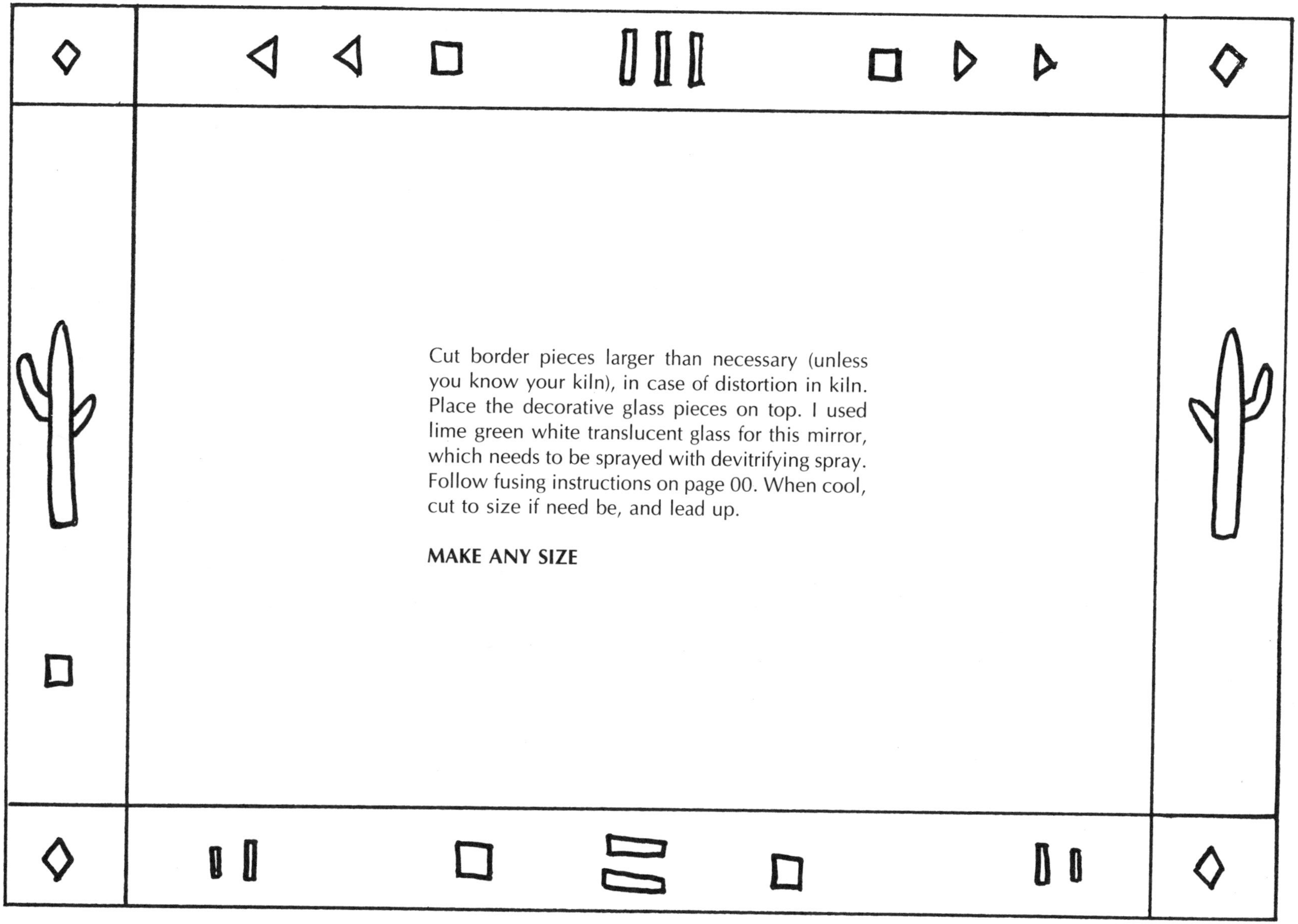

Cut border pieces larger than necessary (unless you know your kiln), in case of distortion in kiln. Place the decorative glass pieces on top. I used lime green white translucent glass for this mirror, which needs to be sprayed with devitrifying spray. Follow fusing instructions on page 00. When cool, cut to size if need be, and lead up.

MAKE ANY SIZE

Red and gold Taj

Illustrated on page 55

Red spectrum is pretty good to fire—it doesn't lose its shape—so cut out according to the pattern. Wash, dry and paint on gold paint for firing, place on prepared kiln shelf, fire up to 720°C (1328°F), or whatever range your particular gold paint needs to be fired to. I used Pollyanna Liquid Bright Gold. When approaching the final temperature check regularly to see if paint has gone shiny, then switch off. When cool, lead up. Solder on hooks and apply felt contact to back of mirror.

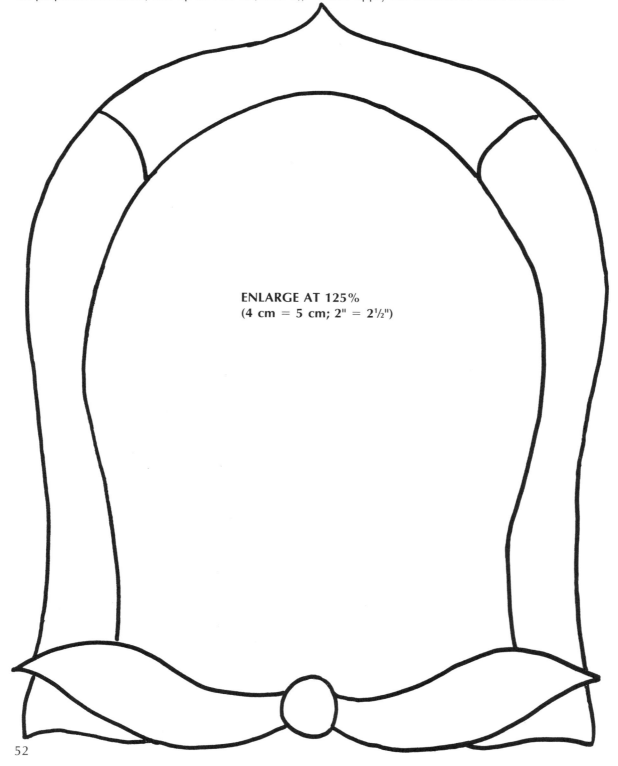

ENLARGE AT 125%
(4 cm = 5 cm; 2" = 2½")

WINDOWS

Kookaburra panels

Illustrated on page 56

Olive green glass is used in the border with 2.5 cm x 2.5 cm
(1" X 1") clear bevels in the diamonds.

The centre design and the inside lines of the gum blossom are
completely foiled and soldered.

In the sidelight the kookaburra's body and the gum blossom are
soldered, and the rest of the panel is leaded, with reinforced border
lead used for the edges.

Floral Gothic window

Illustrated on page 56

Foil and solder all of centre panel and small top
arched piece. Lead up. The outside edge glass was
that beautiful old large hammered glass again.
Check out demolition yards for this glass.

ENLARGE PAGES 54, 57, 58, 59 AT 125%
(4 cm = 5 cm; 2" = 2½")

Section 1

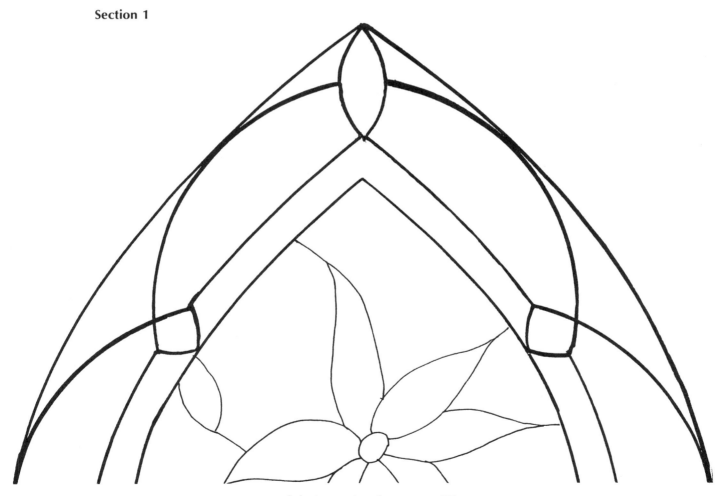

join to section 2 on page 57

*Navajo blanket
mirror (page 47)*

BELOW: *Whispering geckos
mirror (page 50)*

*Blue and White
Indian mirror (page 48)*

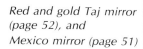

*Red and gold Taj mirror
(page 52), and
Mexico mirror (page 51)*

Floral Gothic window (page 54)

Kookaburra window and side panel (page 53)
Courtesy W. & M. Bidwell

Caladium and peace lily
window (page 60)

join to section 1 on page 54

join to section 3

join to section 2

join to section 4

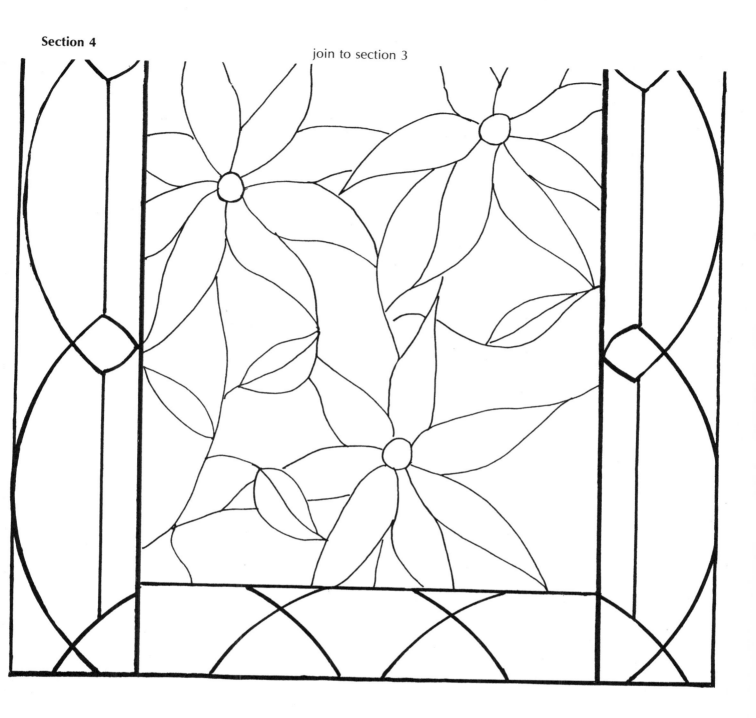

Caladium and peace lily

Illustrated on page 56

A traditionally flavoured panel using flowers from my mother's back verandah; 3 different textured clear glasses add interest to the background.

ENLARGE AT 220%
(2 cm = 4.4 cm; 1" = 2¼")

join

60

join

JEWELLED SUNCATCHERS

Illustrated on inside back cover

ACTUAL SIZE

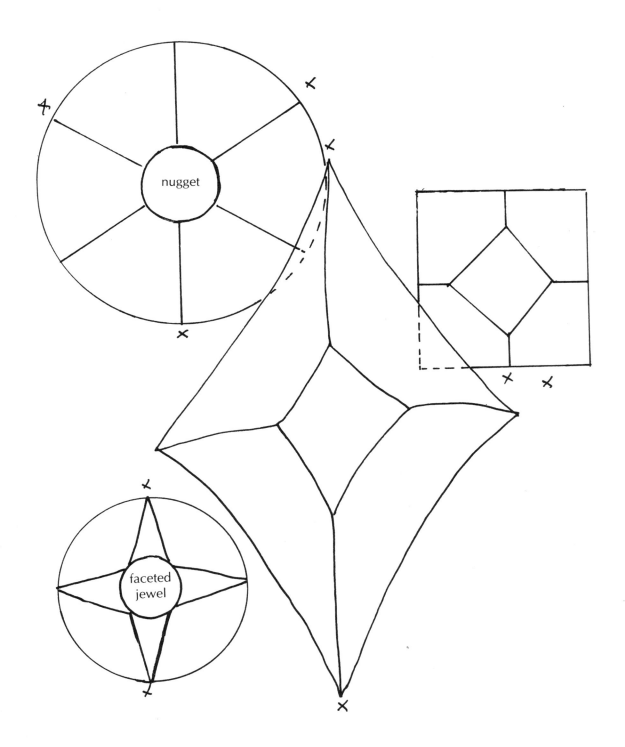

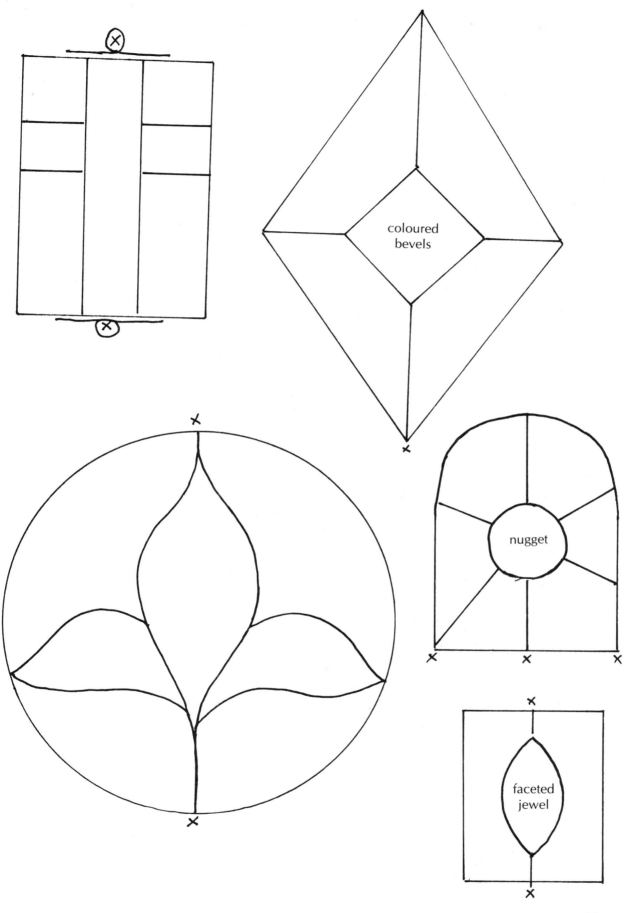

coloured bevels

nugget

faceted jewel

63